RUDYARD KIPLING

Souvenirs of France

Contents

A VERY SHORT INTRODUCTION	1
FRANCE (1913)	3
ONE	6
TWO	26
MY BOY JACK	44
ABOUT THE AUTHOR	45
VERY SHORT CLASSICS	47

A VERY SHORT INTRODUCTION

Rudyard Kipling's relationship with, and affection for, France is not as well documented as that of his with India, but it was a country that played an important role throughout his life.

As a boy of twelve, he accompanied his father to the Paris Exhibition of 1878, where Lockwood Kipling was in charge of the Indian Section of Arts and Manufactures. His father would send him off in the morning with two francs in his pocket and instructions to stay out of trouble. Young Rudyard would spend his money on 'satisfying *déjeuners*' and 'celestial gingerbreads' as well as frequent trips up inside the head of the Statue of Liberty, then part of the Exhibition prior to being shipped to Ellis Island.

He clearly fell in love with the city and its people, returning just over a decade later to find Paris 'much as I had left it, except for an edifice called the Eiffel Tower, but it was still ignorant of wireless and automobiles.' That was soon to change, and Kipling, himself a keen motoring enthusiast, would visit regularly during the rest of his life at the wheel of an automobile for a series of driving holidays.

Memories of these happy times, literary postcards and snapshots, fill the first half of *Souvenirs of France*. The second half is a more sombre and thoughtful affair.

He writes briefly of the First World War – having stayed in the same Swiss hotel as a bunch of German officers in the lead up to hostilities and spending time in France in 1915 – but at more length on its aftermath.

Kipling served on the British Imperial War Graves Commission from 1918 and his work took him to many of the battlefields of the Great War. His only son, John, had died at the Battle of Loos in 1915, just six weeks after his eighteenth birthday, something Kipling does not mention in this book, so the reader can only attempt to imagine how painful and poignant these visits were for him.

He writes of old men and women attempting to fill in trenches with spades, of relatives desperately searching for the bodies of loved ones, of villages destroyed by artillery and of the slow, gradual rejuvenation of the country he so clearly loved.

Souvenirs of France was first published in 1933, one of the last of Kipling's books to appear during his lifetime, and has not been widely available since then.

FRANCE (1913)

Broke to every known mischance, lifted over all
   By the light sane joy of life, the buckler of the Gaul,
   Furious in luxury, merciless in toil,
Terrible with strength that draws from her tireless soil;
Strictest judge of her own worth, gentlest of man's mind,
First to follow Truth and last to leave old Truths behind –
France beloved of every soul that loves its fellow-kind!
Ere our birth (rememberest thou?) side by side we lay
Fretting in the womb of Rome to begin our fray.
Ere men knew our tongues apart, our one task was known –
Each to mould the other's fate as he wrought his own.
To this end we stirred mankind till all Earth was ours,
Till our world-end strifes begat wayside Thrones and Powers –
   Puppets that we made or broke to bar the other's path –
   Necessary, outpost-folk, hirelings of our wrath.
   To this end we stormed the seas, tack for tack, and burst
   Through the doorways of new worlds, doubtful which was first,
   Hand on hilt (rememberest thou?) ready for the blow –
   Sure, whatever else we met, we should meet our foe.
   Spurred or balked at every stride by the other's strength,

So we rode the ages down and every ocean's length!
Where did you refrain from us or we refrain from you?
Ask the wave that has not watched war between us two?
Others held us for a while, but with weaker charms,
These we quitted at the call for each other's arms.
Eager toward the known delight, equally we strove –
Each the other's mystery, terror, need, and love.
To each other's open court with our proofs we came.
Where could we find honour else, or men to test our claim!
From each other's throat we wrenched valour's last reward –
That extorted word of praise gasped 'twixt lunge and guard,
In each other's cup we poured mingled blood and tears,
Brutal joys, unmeasured hopes, intolerable fears –
All that soiled or salted life for a thousand years.
Proved beyond the need of proof, matched in every clime,
O Companion, we have lived greatly through all time!
Yoked in knowledge and remorse, now we come to rest,
Laughing at old villainies that Time has turned to jest;
Pardoning old necessities no pardon can efface –
That undying sin we shared in Rouen market-place.
Now we watch the new year's shape, wondering if they hold
Fiercer lightnings in their heart than we launched of old.
Now we hear new voices rise, question, boast or gird,

As we raged (rememberest thou?) when our crowds were stirred.

Now we count new keels afloat, and new hosts on land,

Massed like ours (rememberest thou?) when our strokes were planned.

We were schooled for dear life's sake, to know each other's blade.

What can Blood and Iron make more than we have made?

FRANCE (1913)

We have learned by keenest use to know each other's mind,
What shall Blood and Iron loose that we cannot bind?
We who swept each other's coast, sacked each other's home,
Since the sword of Brennus clashed on the scales at Rome,
Listen, count and close again, wheeling girth to girth,
In the linked and steadfast guard set for peace on earth!
Broke to every known mischance, lifted over all
By the light sane joy of life, the buckler of the Gaul;
Furious in luxury, merciless in toil,
Terrible with strength renewed from a tireless soil;
Strictest judge of her own worth, gentlest of man's mind,
First to face the Truth and last to leave old Truths behind –
France, beloved of every soul that loves or serves its kind!

ONE

J'étais géant alors, et haut de cent coudées. – BONAPARTE

In the spring of the Paris Exhibition of 1878 my father was in charge of the Indian Section of Arts and Manufactures there, and it was his duty to arrange them as they arrived. He promised me, then twelve or thirteen years old, that I should accompany him to Paris on condition that I gave no trouble. The democracy of an English School had made that easy.

Our happy expedition crossed the Channel in a steamer, I think, made of two steamers attached to each other side by side. (Was it the old *Calais-Douvres* designed to prevent sea-sickness which even the gods themselves cannot do?) And, late at night, we came to a boarding-house full of English people at the back of the Parc Monceau. In the morning, when I had waked to the divine smell of roasting coffee and the bell-like call of the *marchand-d'habits*, my father said in effect, "I shall be busy every day for some time. Here is _____" I think it was two francs. "There are lots of restaurants, all called Duval, where you can eat. I will get you a free pass for the Exhibition and you can go where you please." Then he was swallowed by black-coated officials and workmen in blouses.

Imagine the delight of a child let loose among all the wonders of all the world as they emerged from packing-cases, free to enter every unfinished building that was being raised round an edifice called the Trocadero, and to pass at all times through gates in wooden barricades behind which workmen put up kiosques and pavilions, or set out plants and trees! At first, these genial deep-voiced men asked questions, but after a few days no one looked at my pass, and I considered myself an accepted fly on this great wheel of colour and smells and sights, all revolving to a ceaseless *mitraille* of hammers and machinery. My father, too, had been entirely correct as to this Monsieur Duval. His restaurants were everywhere in Paris; his satisfying *déjeuners* cost exactly one franc. There were also, if one had made the necessary economies, celestial gingerbreads to be bought everywhere.

At the boarding-house were two English boys from a School called Christ's Hospital, or, in talk, the Blue Coat School, which dates from the time of Edward VI. We fraternised, and soon discovered that the Bois de Boulogne was an ideal ground for paper chases, which, at that time, were not understood in France.

But the scholars of Christ's Hospital are obligated to wear the ancient costume of their School. This consists of white linen bands round the neck, in lieu of a collar; a long blue cloth bedgown, fastened by many bright flat buttons and loosely girt at the hip with a leather girdle; blue knee breeches; vividly yellow stockings, and square-toed shoes with buckles. Hats are not worn, and when engaged in athletic exercise the skirts of the blue bedgown are drawn through the girdle. I ask you to consider the effect on a pious *gendarmerie* of two such apparitions, scattering or pursuing trails of torn paper through their sacred Bois in '78! My friends were often halted and questioned; but the gendarmes, tolerant so long as you are polite, soon perceived them to be the young of some species of the insane English. "But what," they demanded unofficially, "is the genesis and intention of this bizarre uniform? Military? Civil? Ecclesiastical?"

My brutal experiments in French among my workmen at my Trocadero made me interpreter here. I have often wondered what the *gendarmes* and the interested priests must have thought. With the ribaldly inquisitive cabmen of those days (they talked too much, those gentlemen in leather hats) one was less polite; for a selection of simple phrases drawn, again, from my blue-bloused friends at the Trocadero, would act on them marvellously. You see, they dared not abandon their vehicles, and the radius of a whiplash is limited. But conceive this against to-day's background! Three small savages capering on, let us say, the *trottoir* of the Avenue d'Iéna while they harpoon a red and roaring *cocher* with epithets of Zoological origin or the ripostes of Cambronne! ... Primitive? Possibly – but Love is founded on a variety of experiences.

When these delights palled, and I had sufficiently superintended my Exposition for the day, I would explore my Paris. Thus I came to know the Bridges and the men who clipped the poodles on the little quays below them. I perceived from the pantomime of the artists engaged that there were two schools of thought in this art. One began at the head; the other at the tail. When I told this to my father, who was also an artist, he laughed enormously. And I accepted it as a tribute to my powers of narration!

I discovered on my own account Quasimodo's Notre Dame. (I believed profoundly in the phantasmagoria of *Notre Dame*, including Esmeralda and her Djali (translated).) I even came to know a little of the Left Bank and the book-boxes of the Quai Voltaire then filled with savage prints and lithographs of the War of '70. The tobacconists, too, sold glazed clay pipes of the heads of bearded soldiers and generals. I considered myself well informed as to that war because, a few years before, I had been given a scrap-book of pictures cut out of the *Illustrated London News*. One was called "The Burning of Bazeilles," and another – a terrible perspective of a forlorn army laying down their rifles in a wilderness of snow – represented Bourbaki's disarmament at the Swiss frontier. The concierge and his wife at the boarding-house also told me tales of that war of which I comprehended – and forgot – nothing.

But my Exposition was always the heart of things for me. A feature of it was the head of Bartholdi's Statue of Liberty which, later, was presented to the United States. One ascended by a staircase (5c.) to the dome of the skull and looked out through the vacant eye-balls at a bright-coloured world beneath. I climbed up there often, and once an elderly Frenchman said to me, "Now, you young Englisher, you can say you have looked through the eyes of Liberty Herself." He spoke less than the truth. It was through the eyes of France that I began to see.

What I did not understand – and it was much – I brought home at evening and laid before my father, who either explained it or told me where I could get the information. He treated me always as a comrade, and his severest orders were, at most, suggestions or invitations. "If I were you, I should do so-and-so" – "You might do worse than, etc." prefaced delightful talks while I was going to bed and he was dressing for some function. It was one of his "suggestions" that led me to look (but not for long) at an Algerian exhibit of educational appliances – copy books filled with classical French sentences, and simple sums perpetrated by young Algerians for whom I felt sympathy, being under a similar yoke. By some means or other I gathered dimly that France "had sound ideas about her Colonies" and that I "might do worse" than remember that. I forgot, of course – to remember later.

This was eight years after the war of '70 and six since the last of the £200,000,000 indemnity had been paid. The Boche had done his best to cripple France, but his memory did not include "the night-cap of Père Bugeaud," nor his prevision anything in the least resembling the Maréchal Lyautey. Madagascar, Tonquin, Indo-China, and the rest were not. The Boche, disregarding the possibilities of a fringe of administration on a beach in North Africa, thought Colonial affairs might divert France. Others must have seen more among the packing-cases where my father talked with the black-coated officials with the rosettes.

I returned to England and my School with a knowledge that there existed a land across the water, where everything was different, and delightful, where one walked among marvels, and all food tasted extremely well. Therefore, I thought well of that place.

Later I was "invited" to study French. "You'll never be able to talk it, but if I were you, I'd try to read it," was his word. I append here the method of instruction. Give an English boy the first half of *Twenty Thousand Leagues under the Sea* in his native tongue. When he is properly intoxicated, withdraw it and present to him the second half in the original. Afterwards – *not* before – Dumas the prince of *amusers*, and the rest as God pleases.

The official study of the French language in the English schools of those days assumed that its literature was "immoral";

whereas the proper slant of accents and the correct assignment of genders was virtuous. In my own interests, then, I made my "graves" and "acutes" as nearly vertical as might be, while my calligraphy served as a fig-leaf to cover those delicate problems of sex in inanimate objects so dear to the meticulous Gaul. During my holidays I would read all the French books that interested, and should not have interested, me, till at sixteen I could deal with them almost as with English.

This served me well a few years later, when, as a subordinate on an Indian journal, it was part of my duty to translate columns upon columns of the *Novoe Vremya* detailing Russian campaigns in Central Asia which were then of some interest. At that time I was a young man in my father's house – a family reunited after long separations in childhood, very content to be together. Never was youth more fortunate! People from all parts of the world would visit my father in his capacity of Provincial Art Director and Curator of the Art Museum. Among these was a French official, or philosopher, named Gustave Le Bon – of the type as it seemed to me of those black-coated ones in Paris six or seven years before. Some of his talk dealt with the significance of those wearisome educational exhibits from Algeria, which I had seen: the theory and the logic of Colonial administration, and so forth, all set out in beautifully balanced French of which the dominant word was "Emprise morale." He talked also on occasion like a Maxim articulate, and my father almost as swiftly, each explaining and comparing the ends and aims of his government. Thus was a second link of the chain riveted which in due time would assist to draw my heart towards France.

Occasionally Russian officers wandered through our part of Northern India who spoke admirable French and explained disarmingly their innocent missions. And there was an annually recurrent native theatrical troupe that presented Indian plays in the bazaar, whose elderly and unshaven German scene-painter had been, he told me, "out on the barricades in '48." He revealed to me a France I have never imagined.

In the Anglo-Indian life of those days were no theatres; no picture galleries; no cinemas; no transport other than the horse; and no society. Every one was either an official or a soldier, with his work to do. Our community numbered in the hot weather perhaps seventy whites in all. At the big Christmas dances, when the outlying stations came in, four hundred might be present for a week! The climate, through half the year, forbade exercise after seven in the morning and before six in the evening. There was time, then, to read – anything and everything one could find – from Scarron's dreary *Roman Comique* to Gyp, as well as that ponderous *Novoe Vreyma* and the French papers. The journals in our office came in from Paris to Pekin; each wonderfully preserving its own national smell, so that one could identify it in the dark. At that time – '83 to '88 – the French press was not nationally enamoured of England. I answered some of their criticisms by what I then conceived to be parodies of Victor Hugo's more extravagant prose. The peace of Europe, however, was not seriously endangered by these exercises; my illustrious contemporaries must have known that newspapers have to be filled daily.

Oh! Demain c'est la grande chose!
De quoi demain sera-t-il fait?
VICTOR HUGO

After these happy years, I found myself again in Paris at the

ONE

Exhibition of 1889-90. My city was much as I had left it, except for an edifice called the Eiffel Tower, but it was still ignorant of wireless and automobiles. I used to establish myself at a small hotel in the Batignolles, dominated by a fat elderly landlady who brought me unequalled *café au lait* in big bowls. I must have made other friendships also – else how did I come to assist at that moonlight *pas de quatre* in front of the Sorbonne? A glance into the future would have shown me that I was to be a Doctor of that learned Institute, but I needed all my eyes at the time to watch a *gendarme* who desired to attach himself to our company merely because we sang to him that Love was an infant of Bohemia ignorant of the Code Napoléon.

Those times passed also, and life became more varied. It included a certain amount of travel – to South Africa for example, where at a town called Johannesburg I had the honour of meeting some German officers, unnecessarily interested in the future political relations and armaments, which last their country supplied, of the Boers. They talked too loudly. Personally, I have always liked the Boer, and it occurred to me, as to some others, at the time that he might not be our most serious opponent.

During the Boer War (1899-1902) what should have enlightened us all to the future was the thoroughness of the anti-British propaganda, much of which rebounded mainly from the United States by way of what was vaguely called "The Continent". Some of it was of French provenance – grossly impolite and playing into the Boches' hands. But the specific charges of our "atrocities" during the war revealed, though we had not sense enough to profit by it, the Boche mentality. For example, there was a statement that on a certain day, at a certain place, some English officers entered a Boer farmhouse which was flying the white flag. Names and dates were entirely true. (I was with the party and "shared" the honours of the action.) It went on to say that we had dragged out two or three Boer men and women from under their beds there; had given them a hundred yards' allowance and shot them down as they ran! In other words, it prefigured absolutely the technique of Louvain and Termonde and the villages of the Border in '14, etc., etc.; the touch about the "hundred yards' allowance" being a sporting attempt to dress the dish à l'anglaise. Another announcement – a telegraphic "extra" – picked up on the floor of a newspaper office in Bloemfontein the day after we had entered that town, affirmed that our Brigade of Guards had, two days previously, been driven on to the attack in one of their "battles" of those days, by the fire of their own Corps Artillery! Even so, we were not enlightened; and when later we came across very deep trenches, undercut, on the shrapnel side, no one realised we were looking at the forerunner of the "dug-out" and a new type of war. But how could we guess?

The Boer wisely did not care to sit in trenches as the German experts had recommended. He preferred to lie behind a boulder in the open and shoot his picked man at eight hundred or a thousand yards. When he had expended his cartridges he retired towards the Equator on his indefatigable little pony. The uniformed foreign volunteers of the forces (there was no uniform among the Boers) had been trained in an older school. Consequently they were sometimes captured or even killed in action. Among our "captives" was a charming Frenchman who had fought because he intensely loathed the English. He was master of a pleasant literary style, and in his account, later, of his adventures referred to me (surely Hate is more observant than love!) by the one title to which I most objected. If he be still alive I would make him my compliments across the years and assure him that his thrust went home.

But I go forward too quickly. The business of Fashoda in '98 was – after the French Press had been very rude, very stupid and very short-sighted in beating us to help "the King of Prussia" – the opening of the inevitable *entente cordiale*. At the time the French Government, I think, purchased a quantity of military stores which were duly expended sixteen years later in quite another direction. And in 1915, in a vast hollow of the Argonne, I beheld an army of forty thousand men and a hundred and twenty Seventy-Fives reviewed by Joffre and Kitchener, and felt the *frisson* run through its ranks when Kitchener shook hands with and talked to General Marchand in the face of the line. Then the bank of horizon-blue and the clanking guns rolled forward to the unsatisfied thunders beyond the horizon.

After the Boer War, but the precise date has escaped me, there visited Cape Town, where I used to spend my winters, the triple-screw cruiser *Dupleix* (Admiral Rivet) which was thrown open to all the world for "inspections". There are two ways of "inspecting" ships. The first is to go round the ship before taking *déjeuner* on board. The second is to sit quite still after *déjeuner* on board, and let the ship go round you. Since the lighter guns of the *Dupleix* were mounted by threes in little cupolas, the impression of her revolving armament was prodigious. Cape Town, in turn, invited all her officers to "inspect" the vineyards of Constantia, where they make not too weak wines. My charge, on that occasion, was a young Breton lieutenant. He returned, his head on his companion's shoulder, sleeping like an angel. You must understand I had several times drunk to the *entente cordiale* in sweet champagne at eleven in the morning on the deck of the *Dupleix*; temperature beneath her awnings about

85°F. Thus honour was satisfied!

But in all those years I knew little of France beyond an occasional trip to Paris. The coming of the automobile broke the spell, and, year after year, in the cars of the period when motorists were as much pioneers of travel as are now airmen, we explored France. ("But, Monsieur, we cannot accommodate *that* here. It will frighten the horses!" That was at the old hotel in Avignon.)

Then was revealed to us, season after season, the immense and amazing beauty of France; the laborious thrift of her people, and a little of their hard philosophy; the excellence of her agriculture and the forethought and system of her forestry. Some of our Indian forestry officials had had their training at Nancy, and had always told me about it.

But at first one paid for one's knowledge with one's skin. Neither men nor beasts were prepared for this visitation of ferocious and exacting vehicles; and part of the tourists' equipment used to be a whip with a long lash, to save the temperamental dogs of France from committing suicide. The soft roads of the astonished departments went to pieces beneath our very bad tyres, and we broke our strongest springs on humpbacked little bridges in secluded towns of one street, where the old women knitted at the fountains. (That was the Rhone Road. Route 7.) Worst of all, we were so ignorant that we did not know that one always finds a good *déjeuner* if one falls in behind the French Army at half-past eleven.

But matters adjusted themselves with the years and, from the point of view of the early motorists, civilisation no horribly overruns France and one eats, instead of dines, at "hotels of all the luxuries".

There is a certain little meadow by the sea, under Mount

Canigou, which Spring fills with narcissi when she first sets foot in Europe. For years in succession we went down to that meadow, spread our maps among the flowers, and began our travels – all France to play with, and our auto to convey us. From the tourists' point of view March is not a good season. Winds blow; there may be snow-drifts on the low passes that a month later would be clear. Yet, for those who love the land and its people, March is the month above all; for then France, who never stops working, begins her spring cleanings, loppings and prunings. The road-men are out taking stock of winter damages; the happy, dirty gipsy-vans are out too; the barges along a thousand miles of canals refit and repaint under the eye of the barge-dogs, who allow no liberties; the roads are made interesting by the dung-carts, the huge bundles of new vine-stocks, and the freshly ordered bright-painted agricultural implements. The working year renews its pulse with the roar almost of a tide.

One blemish remains. No motorist can foresee what any citizen of the Republic on foot will do. He is generally at work in the fields, but when he walks the roads he is a flickering, wanton mystery.

I have seen him absorbed in dreams, with expanded chest and radiant eye, advance well on the wrong side of the road, till our horn made him leap sideways and call us "Assassin!"

But a people who work as unrelentingly as the French, must have great dreams to salt their lives with. When a man has spent the long day leading pannier loads of manure, a donkey-load at a time, up the terraced hillside to his hanging vineyard; when he has hand-dealt each knotted vine-stock its own portion of the good dark muck, it is then he wants to straighten his back on the way home, and to plunge into the life of events and prodigies – such as lecturing his wife or being President of the Republic.

I tried to explain to a companion of one of our tours that these "play-acting people", as he called them, have lived through devastating dramas of their own, the consequences of which lie heavy on every aspect of their lives. We had gone astray one evening in a wild plain of heath and rock. Darkened by olive trees and lit by the flare of a windy sunset. We came into a village where a line of young men, linking hands, swept the public square dancing. Their faces were very clear in that unearthly light, and the tricolour ribbons in their caps rattled in the mistral. An infantry soldier leaned against a shop door and watched them with an elder brother's instructed smile.

"What's the circus?" said my friend as they shouted round us.

"Those are conscripts," I replied. "Young men drawn for service in the Army for the next three years." But he was frankly contemptuous, and the lounging infantryman only impressed him as slovenly and un-groomed.

"But there are three-quarters of a million of them," I said. "They have to take over each other's clothes and equipment and wear them out – like monks. Very little is wasted in this country." All the English in him revolted at the apparent meanness, but the splendour of the sacrifice was hid. As a Frenchman once said to me: "We Continentals are more separated from your world by our compulsory service than by anything else. How can you English understand our minds if you do not realise those years of service – those years of service for us all? When we come to talk to you about life it is like talking about death to children."

Again – at a cosmopolitan dinner party – an Italian youth, but so English-trained that the young Englishman he was talking

ONE

to looked on him as a brother, said, all of a sudden, "Yes, it *was* rather a bore! I had got my House colours and I had got my Boats. I'd have given *anything* for another year at Eton. But I had to come away for my service. Get up at three in the morning and groom your own horse, you know, and all that sort of thing. The pay is a penny a day and the food – you can't live on it!…"

The Englishman stared – it was having to give up the Boats that impressed him, but a young Frenchman who had done his time merely nodded. I have been privileged also to hear a foreign professor of some ideal or other explain to a rather prominent philosopher that he "guessed France lacked a certain seriousness of moral purpose." To whom the philosopher, looking back across the years: "Ye-es. I did my service with the Artillery." Who would more surely extract fun, irony, and their true taste out of things as they pass, than one who had been forced to live under bodily stress in the face of fact, to sweat and pant and cast him down in the mud, dust, and heat of manoeuvres – a unit among many thousands?

And as one came to know France more intimately one gathered memories and pictures of people and things which became part of one's accepted life, destined to grow more significant through the years.

On the way to Lavandou, before Lavandou had been exploited, there stood against a belt of pines, an old black barn whose door carried a torn placard of some Government loan, which resembled a grotesque profile. This was a landmark always joyously greeted because it marked for us a stage of our great journey from Spring's Own Meadow. That placard survived all the war – always preserving its comic appearance. It outlived all the millions of the dead and the hundreds of murdered villages.

At Rheims, which was one of our northerly circuits, we used to buy candles to burn before Joan of Arc. "But what do *you* want with candles?" the sacristan would say. (The God who made all the Creeds knew, but we did not.) And, two years after our last visit together in peace time, there remained only the gutted shell of the Cathedral, but, in a corner of the void, lay a metal candle-holder – I tried to believe that very one on which we had spiked our useless offerings.

Whatever the sacristan may think, I believe in the miracle that Joan of Arc wrought for France through the bad years of 1903-7, when the children born or begotten under the shadows of the '70 war had come to manhood and were (it will happen again in France as it will in England) full of defeatism and that costive ill-will that crawls like a snapping cur on the heels of war. Scientific observers may argue that those years also preluded the entry of young France into the arena of sports. It is incontestable that, more and more at the epoch, ere the kiosques filled with little weekly papers of athletic interest: more and more did one meet in the roads young men training severely for walking, running, or cycle contents. But, *pari passu*, I observed in the churches that Saint Joseph was everywhere being dispossessed from his shrine in favour of Joan of Arc. It is not the sporting journals but to Joan that I ascribe the renaissance of strength and purpose in the young of France at that hour.

With one exception – and he was a *douanier* fortified with brandy against the terrible rain of the Nord – I have in twenty-five years' road-travel met nothing but kindness and prompt help from every one – even from my ancient friends, the *gendarmes*.

Had I space, or you patience, I could tell you of the Personal

ONE

Devil of Marsillargues, and of Michael Coste, the village electrician there who saved us from him; of the Boy of Villers Bocage who will unquestionably be the second Lesseps of France; of the veteran of '70, on the road to Canigou, who kept bees, and who talked and looked precisely like Anatole France; of the rural postman, survivor of a Madagascar battalion of '83-'86 ("Eighty of us, Monsieur, returned out of eleven hundred"), who delivered the superb lecture on the late Mr. Wilson, at the bridge below Bluebeard's Castle; and of the Lady of Bordeaux who, dressed almost entirely in one hat, also lectured the two embarrassed *gendarmes* (Do you know that the Bordelais can blush?) and the unembarrassed cab-driver.

At every turn of my ways I gathered a certain amount of knowledge, and, perhaps, a little understanding.

For example, only a few years ago in the Béarnaise, on a hot day – the car halted opposite the house of a big-boned farmer standing by his splendid reversible plough. Behind him, his silky plough bullocks filed in to their dark stalls for the noontide rest.

"Are Monsieur and Madame interested in beasts? Good. Come and look."

We were presented to each darling by name. It was a thriving establishment with the usual notice of a Government loan on a barn door. Then, underneath a wall by the main road, we saw an infant of four armed with a little green-barked switch which some one had peeled into pretty patterns for him. His office was to keep a flock of baby turkeys in the shadow of that wall as the sun shifted. "Sun is bad for young turkeys," the farmer observed. "But *he* knows! He knows all about it. If you took his stick away he'd cry. Wouldn't thee?"

The babe did not answer. His eyes were on his flock as it

piped and cowered beneath the menace of his sceptre. *They* knew all about it too.

"Your son?"

"Assuredly." With an arm over the forequarters of an ox who stood as still as a mantelpiece, the farmer talked of "La Terre" and the obligations of those who served it to enter on their vows early.

It was good stuff – well delivered – and impressive in what it took for granted. I dare not paint the horror of an English Administration and all its paid officials if an infant were discovered to be employed in what is legally "agricultural labour".

But the strength of France is in her soil. If you stood one hundred Frenchmen on their heads, you would find the good plough-mould on the boots of at least seventy-five. They have known in their boyhood the chill before sunrise, and the cool of the evening on the naked chest; the sight, sound, and smell of the worked earth; the hot, dry, rustling cornland before the reapers go in; and the secrets of the dark and tempting barns. They give to La Terre the reverence they deny to some other gods: and she repays their worship.

There is a town by a great River, where they hold agricultural shows on the main boulevard, attaching electric-power wires casually to the tree-trunks, with no more protection than an occasional warning that, if you touch them you will perish. (With us, a pensioned Civil Servant would guard every one.) They sell, under the cool shadows of the trees, fascinating farm appliances from bee-hives to wine-presses. Once I asked an agent how long a certain manure-pump would last – *marche* being the word I used. The answer was illuminating. "If you leave it lying out in the winters, as you English do, it will not *marche* more than two years. Give it shelter and it will *marche* for ten." That is the truth. No one can calculate how much the English farmer loses by sheer neglect of his tools, and by sloth at the careless end of the day or season.

And in this same town is a flower-market, where each morning people attend whose little carts are drawn by dogs. The first business of every dog is to assure himself that all his friends and enemies in the square are present. To each, then, the proper word. That delivered, each dog lies down under his cart in silence till market closes and all go home. I was interested in a largish, square-mouthed, black fellow, whose zeal to arrive was only equalled by his choking anxiety to get away. I would have talked to him, but he told me he was responsible for the cart, and was devoid of social accomplishments.

Afterwards, I foregathered with an old man who carried baggage from the railway station to quiet boarding-houses. His team was a fawn-coloured lady of seven varieties, fresh from maternal duty, and a composite black-and-white pointer. They were delivering a portmanteau at the time, and with some parade; for the lady who received it was evidently friend of all three. "Yes," said the old man when she had gone. "These two mix themselves in all my affairs. It gives them importance. As guard-dogs, of course, they are useless. They would not interfere with any one because, you see, *any one* may come out to take a trunk. In *our* business we must ingratiate ourselves with our *clientèle*." (The bitch fawned and feathered round my knees for proof of it.) "Other dogs are different? That is true! You tried to talk to that black one in the Flower Market? *But* he was in sole charge of his cart! Monsieur, it may serve you to remember that you should never speak to a single dog on duty. Two perhaps may be polite, but one … not so often."

Then he showed me how his team could pull on demand, going up hill.

"In theory why should a dog work at all?" I demanded.

"It is not a theory. It is logic. Because a dog is an animal of intelligence. He knows right and wrong – especially injustice. He loves a position of trust. It gives him a point of honour – his opportunity for devotion. Like a woman in effect. Now, *she* here has three little ones at home. She will feed them at *déjeuner* of course. But if I left her behind afterwards, she would bite *him* when he came back. Just like a woman again! Logically, also, dogs are too wise to be idle. It is an insult to them."

It cannot be easy to overthrow a people whose men, women, and children, and dogs look on work as a natural part of life. With this virtue goes an acceptation of thrift in all things, which makes most things easy.

Again an illustration. At a big Paris post office a messenger entered to cash a money order and turned away from the wicket leaving one sou lying on the counter. The postal employé who had cashed him the order was serving another customer and did not notice. But two well-dressed women in the queue instantly warned the messenger of his oversight, in that strict sudden staccato which a Frenchwoman reserves for serious affairs. It was not the amount that mattered but the principle. Call it sou-mindedness if you will. Myself, I respect it.

It makes for simplicity; the acceptance of hard living which fortifies the moral interior as small pebbles assist the digestion of fowls; and it allows its practitioner to be as extravagant as he pleases in speech and oratory. (The Englishman's inveterate habit of waste explains his inveterate habit of understatement.)

In the course of these years it occurred to me that there existed in France a civilisation at least coeval with ours; equally complete – not to say contented with itself; as incomprehensible as ours but complementary. What of civilisation since the fall of Rome had evolved itself appeared to me to have been due to one or other of those influences; the later systems being predatory, parvenu, or imposed. Therefore, what of civilisation was to continue, lay in our united hands.

This idea precipitated itself out of talks, and experiences trivial or grave, the first part of which I have set down here.

TWO

Et ce n'est pas une vigilance d'un jour qui nous est demandée. Qui donc pourrait mesurer l'ampleur des oscillations auxquelles cette guerre a donné cours, ou prédire en quelles limites de temps pourra s'enclore l'évolution des conditions de vie mondialement successivement changées? – GEORGES CLEMENCEAU

France still remembers (but we have forgotten) how the shadow of war darkened over Europe from 1907 onwards when the watchword "World-Dominion or Downfall" was written, taught, prayed, preached, sculptured, set to music, and legislated for as a Gospel, an end, and a certainty. Part of my winters I then used to spend at a "sports" hotel in Switzerland frequented by German officers. On the day of their Kaiser's birthday, they would dine – very well – and talk and sing of The Day with great clarity and many threats against all mankind. And not the officers alone. I recall, out of many, an interesting conversation with a most respectable Town Councillor of Hamburg. He laid down for me the minimum of his country's requirements from England. They included an "order" by the "English Parliament" to our "Colonies" to abolish all tariffs against his country, etc., etc. Failing this, the English were to beware of the "Furor Teutonicus" – as it might have been *Ira Normanorum*. It was illuminating; it was as plain as the Boche Press, or the way in which the German Colonies were armed and used as points of friction and blackmail all over the world. That was before Agadir. Could France or England say they had not been warned? ...

What the French preparations were is known to us. The English argument was: *"Fi de manteau quad il fait beau."* Peace being one hundred years old must, they said, be in the immutable order of "Civilisation." It followed, then, that even to teach respectable Englishmen to stand and walk without falling over each other and themselves was not only absurd but impious. Had we not an immediately effective Army of 80,000 as well as some Field Artillery? In view of the claims of "social reform" on the national purse, what more could be reasonably asked? Those were the years of nightmare!

In '13–'14 there was little pretence or concealment. The vital question was England's attitude. This was put to me, baldly enough, in a little hotel in Central France by a colonel of the 29th of the Line. He said, above a map, indicating the very place, "If you do not prolong our left *here*, you will also perish!" An Englishman who overheard him, remarked, "That man seemed very full of something or other. What was that *goshe* (gauche) he was talking about?"

By chance or coincidence, it was about that time – late '13 or spring of '14 – that I met again in Paris Monsieur Gustave Le Bon. It was as though the wheel had come full circle after thirty years. So, naturally, instead of questioning the future at the pleasant meal, we talked of the past.

A little later, in the hot staleness of an alternately chained and unchained newspaper's office[1], an old man said to me, "It is for now! *They* will obey their orders. *We* shall not obey even ourselves." But Monsieur Clemenceau forgot that he had been Mayor of Montmartre during the Siege of '70 when, on his notification, the children of the quarter went to school through the shells.

Nor did he foresee that it would be laid upon him very soon to save his country.

* * *

My next visit to France was at the harvest time in the autumn of '15. The little Algerian copy-books had borne fruit in many places. There were multitudes of trains filled with Algerians, Senegalese, and Moroccan troops, commanded by a type of officer new to me and yet indescribably familiar since it handled native troops and delivered low-voiced orders in tongues whose cadence and inflection seemed on the point of giving me their meaning. I asked if there were any difficulty as to Muhammedan food on campaign. I understood that they had not time to consider these things, but, in the case of stricter sects, sheep and goats were killed after the orthodox Moslem fashion. Yes, so far as was known, all was quiet in North Africa. A man (Lyautey was the name) was in charge yonder, and there was also a certain quantity of wheat ready to ship to France when needed. A bearded, pale-eyed youth, older than his tortured years, told me this in the wreck of a courtyard while the remnant of a native battalion, just come out of action, cooked the evening

---

[1] This refers to a newspaper edited by Monsieur Clemenceau which was always in difficulties with the French Government of the day.

meal over fires, as in an Indian caravanserai.

In other places, I saw descendants of my old landlady of the Batignolles – slippered, untidy, voluble – dealing out bowls of soup to the *poilus*, or driving cows in ploughs not too far behind the shells. That is why I desire a colossal statue on one of the Seine bridges to that enduring woman who also stood fast and said: *"Faut pas s'en faire."*

Of the men and officers of the French Army, it seemed to me that the demands of their normal national life had spared them some of the subconscious unease that weighed on our people. Accustomed by heredity and training to the food, exposure, and wasted hours at manoeuvres, to lack of privacy and the impact of crowds, they were released from too much desire to dwell on the emotions of civil life. Compare the verse and prose written by combatants of the two races, and you will, I fancy, see a difference[2].

On the other hand, the French were in their own country and sometimes very near their own homes. In war, as in love, the divided objective leads to the Devil. There was a young soldier from Amiens where his girl also lived. His battalion came, at last, to lie within a few kilometres of the town. Twice he deserted, and twice France, who understands humanity, overlooked it.

---

[2] The two schools are alike, it seems to me, in the sincere angularity of rigidity of their literary frame-work. Is this because the writers had lived for years among naked beams, and girders, shattered walls, and harshly interrupted outlines? Their insistence on obscure personal moods and minute phenomena observed at close range, was explained to me by a man who said that, when one lies for hours under machine-gun fire in a shell-hole or a tobacco field, one concentrates, for sanity's sake, on the veining of some single leaf; the union of two water drops; or the slow deliquescence of mud which releases a pebble on the slope of a crater. The result appears in the verses. It may be so.

The third time he was shot in a little chalk-pit within sight of the Amiens road. I had the tale from a child, who told it as savages tell – without comment.

And here is another tale, the authenticity of which I have not yet arrived at. It is ascribed to a General of the kind which is everywhere at unexpected hours. Very early one morning he came across a firing-party, etc., on their way to duty. The condemned had been found asleep, worn out, on sentry in a front-line trench. The General, who knew his dossier, said to him, "You do not die because of any disgraceful act on your part; but because your death will save the lives of others. It takes more of courage to die thus. So, I will come with you." His arm around the man, the General accompanied him, and, just before those eyes ceased to see, saluted. There are several Generals whom I could credit with such an act, but I should like to know who it was[3].

* * *

At last there arrived what was called – too justly, as one sees now – an Armistice; and the late President Woodrow Wilson entered to create a new world for us, with no authority whatever from his countrymen to make any arrangements in his name. (His political party was, at the moment, if I remember, in a electoral minority of 1,200,000 votes.)

His countrymen, through their representatives, repudiated, therefore, all the arrangements that he had made. These would have pledged England and the U.S.A. to assist France in event of future German attack, and would have stabilised the future.

---

[3] I have since learned it was the late General Maud'huy.

TWO

But a people whose origins, *ex necessitate*, must have abjured, individually and in writing, all European connections, do not readily embrace external responsibilities. The United States cleared her skirts of the imbroglio with the alacrity of a shocked schoolmistress. Ethnologically this was inevitable; objectively it was very comic; but, in its consequences, never was so far-reaching a refusal nor confusion more incalculable.

Yes, remember, the importation of the United States into the war was due to our common faults – our common inadequate preparations; our divided counsels and our national follies.

There followed, presently, a passionate propaganda that "Civilisation" should "put Germany on her feet" because she was in economic ruin and her heart had changed. After "Civilisation" had sufficiently studied that ruin and satisfied herself, at some cost, of the worthlessness of German currency, the mark returned to parity as a machine-gun re-hoists itself over the apparently abandoned trench. The manoeuvre to abolish her internal debt cost Germany no more than a few thousand old and unusable persons wiped out, perhaps by starvation. It was magnificent, and it was the first step of the real war which began at a quarter-past eleven on the 11th November 1918.

* * *

My duties as one of the British Imperial War Graves Commission took me for the next few years over the devastated areas – from that obliteration of all things which had been the Ypres Salient to all but obliterated Rheims, of whose fifteen thousand houses thirty-five, I think, remained intact.

At first the Commission's great camions, equipped like ships, would push out into oceans of weeds to discover where lay the rough cemeteries of the early years. They would be guided sometimes by voices out of the earth from beneath indistinguishable bivouacs, saying: "Monsieur, this was Flers," or whatever might be the name of the wreckage that had once carried a name.

And one met faces that seemed as though fire had passed over them – faces that hurried from one place to another asking for news of relatives – of women and children – who had utterly disappeared during the German "occupations". What would have been the effect on British mentality if even one hundred civilians had "disappeared" after a raid in England? And what if all the country between Canterbury and Bournemouth had been passed through a sieve for four years?

Then there came up out of that soil of France which had made them, old men and women, each with a long-handled spade, to refill the trenches, and the gun-pits. One was never out of sight of these labouring couples. At Rheims they impeded the Annamites and Senegalese who coiled away the endless barbed-wire. At Soissons and the border towns eastward, they assisted the removal of debris from the suburbs thus: "But this is *our* land. Look! Here was our garden. Here was the well. Monsieur, *mon Capitane*, *we* tell *you* that *this* is *our* land." And all along the Somme, where troops gathered and exploded waste ammunition in the bellowing pits and hollows, they laboured like their own lost oxen with almost as little head for other interests. Theirs seemed an impossible task, even in the second year when the earth began to be cicatrised with white sutures to prove that the gaping trenches were satiated.

One followed these labours as the inadequate passenger seconds, with useless movements of shoulders and feet, the efforts of his chauffeur. It was like a relief after the toothache when the first milliner's shop, with new hats, reopened in a small town near Laventie, which for years had resembled a decayed jaw-bone packed with green teeth.

The devastations were so scientific that one could convey no idea of them to visiting strangers. They would look at a smear of triturated brick-dust on an expanse of pitted mud and say: "But do you mean to tell me that there was ever anything there at all?" I imagine this was one of the reasons why an English expert, from whom we seem destined still to suffer, pronounced at the Paris Conference that the French had *"effrontément exagéré les revendications des régions dévastées."*

In this wandering employ one came upon very many people seen unguarded in their heights and deeps, from every angle of despair, sleek profiteering, resolution, stunned agony, and almost insane cynicism. Often, too, in hideously ludicrous predicaments. There was a point near some brick-fields where our armies had once touched and where the dead lay close. A French officer – too young for that work – was dealing with the human debris. To him came an elderly widow (for the moment mad) in search of her husband's body. It was there, she said. Her business was to find it. Tenderly and repeatedly, the young man explained that such matters were not to be looked upon, even could she indicate the very spot. She did not hear him. The trench must be searched from end to end. She would wait. At least, when the horror of appeal and denunciation had passed all limit, a woman of the people led her away. The boy wiped his forehead and gasped – "It is not fair. It is not fair. But it is always happening!" In other places, the peasant women sold butter and eggs to other searchers for the dead, and religiously cheated them at every small turn. Then they would give up half a day in which they might have continued their practices, to gather and walk five miles with flowers to lay on some grave of our people. Equally devout in both duties. After all, mankind is but made of earth and water; and our hearts, like muddy streams, cleanse themselves as they go forward.

The two races had been utterly wearied of each other's enforced society through four years. (Think how one sickens after four hours in an overcrowded railway compartment!) There were a thousand points of friction and disagreement. But I think that the detail of that *chiffonage* along the empty fronts acted as an anodyne. And I know that when a French mining company reinstalled its machinery on a site churned thirty feet deep by the gun-fire of years, they came on what remained of two of our dead. They halted everything, and – the great girders for the engine-beds hanging in the cranes – sent word ten miles to notify our people to take delivery.

* * *

In '20 and '21 it seemed as though all the Muhammedan world was about to range itself against Western civilisation, and England in particular. At one point only the ring of menace was incomplete. France was not then passionately loyal to British interests in the East – so I asked questions. I was assured that there was nothing of importance stirring in any French Muhammedan zone. All sorts of native troops had, of course, been demobilised lately in North Africa. Doubtless some of them had gone home with a revolver or so in view of social engagements *en route*. And, perhaps, might have held up some tourists. But why not go and look – at the Department of Algiers, for instance?

TWO

So I crossed to the Department of Algiers and found myself returned to a people almost identical in aspect, habit, and gesture with the Moslems among whom I had been brought up. But I understood not a word of their speech. It was like a dream in which one can only make signs to old friends.

They were serenely occupied with their own affairs, into which, it appeared, the French entered as not too exacting comrades. Much of the administration seemed casual and desultory – yet reaching its end as a French infantry attack drifts to the objective. There was a sufficiency, too, of that officialdom and legality with which the national genius adorns the façades of its administration; but one felt that it could be more easily outflanked here than in other lands. The mystery baffled me. Let us concede that Islam in Africa is more homogeneous, less disorientated by the proximity of caste, than Islam in Asia. Granted that there are no organised bodies of public opinion in France to advocate the claims of the ineffective in order to justify their own inefficiencies. Granted, though Colonial officials deny this, that Paris does not eternally and infernally interfere with the man on the spot. Even so, how is the indescribable ease – *détente* if that be the right word – of the administrative atmosphere reached and maintained? How is the parallelism of the two races achieved, so that one does not make, nor the other demand, allowances? I fell back on Gustave Le Bon's formula delivered thirty-five years before: *"C'est l'emprise morale."* Those little copy-books of my Exposition had done their work.

(I suppress here – though it was very beautiful – a denunciation of certain French writers who would represent their Colonial officers as mournfully devoured, beneath tropical moons, by a passion for drugs and fat black females.)

A Mayor of Algiers who held the city both in and by the hand told me a secret. "It is Paris," said he, "upon whom we depend in the last resort for some of our diplomacy. Our Algerian Deputies go there, of course, to take their seats in the Chambers. Many of our people know Paris, and more since this war. Good! If any important man out there," he pointed largely towards the Niger, "feels restless, or neglected, or thinks he would like to be a Prophet, he can always visit Paris. It is only a few days away. Perhaps he is invited there to talk. So he goes. For the rest? – oh! Paris charges herself with *that*! And he comes back more contented."

I had never thought of so simple a device! Were I a potential Mahdi with a grievance, the spectacle of the Place de la Concorde flood-lit in a May night would exercise a certain influence on me also.

* * *

Beyond a tourist's experience of Algiers and an interesting night in microscopical, but aggressively French, Chandernagore where defaulting debtors from Calcutta used to take refuge, I know nothing of French colonies. But one result of the labours there was delivered to me *en bloc*, at the French Colonial Exposition only three years ago, where the illuminated splendour and mystery of the Ang-Kor façade imposed its significance upon the most hardened.

For me, once again, the wheel of life came full circle. Vincennes had been no part of my Paris: but the packing-cases; the rosetted officials running everywhere to overtake or countermand instructions; the furious erection of the stalls of the concessionaires (their sweetmeats were not so satisfying as in '78); the smell of trampled turf, raw timber, and sweating workmen, filled me with the august pride of a proprietor. And when I was told of the annoying little *contretemps* and delays, "incidental to all expositions but which would not interest you, Monsieur," I kept my face and pretended complete detachment.

Also, I was talking with ghosts – good and justified shadows out of that past when a few bewildered Africans and some copy-books were all that France showed the world of her Colonies. And now, at every turn – easy, assured, and interested – I beheld her peoples of many races and lands. They were each integral and unquestioning parts of a system which had been worked out on the line laid down long ago. One heard the triumphant ghosts summarising it. Listen! "Ye-es. You might do worse than look at the educational show-case. The French have some sound notions about their Colonies." … "My dear *confrère*, I tell you we must act so as to assimilate and to civilise those races according to the measure of *their* capacities. *Not* ours! It is not so? He there – that boy of yours – may see it perhaps, but not we."

* * *

As it is, I am well content with the multitude of beautiful things found by chance in small local museums, in neglected churches, in villages beneath unadvertised chateaux which do not yet sell as postcards. There is richer treasure of this sort in France than with us – perhaps because their rulers in the past, when they felt religious or angry, merely slew men. Ours, more respectable, contented themselves with murdering the irreplaceable work of artists. I went, several times, in search of the plunder of the eye, with a friend whose passion was thirteenth-century glass of a blue which is now restricted to the Angels. We discovered one very small, very accessible window in a decayed little church which we thought might be exchanged for something really modern and artistic from Limoges, or even Theirs. But it appears that these trifles are known and recorded – probably by the Church: certainly by the Police. So all the glass I possess now is one of those rings which the *poilus* used to make out of material that fell into their hands at Rheims.

And, because I said that the brick bulk of Albi Cathedral, seen against the moon, hit the soul like a hammer, my friend showed me vast cold Byzantine cathedrals where no one seemed to enter except, at its hour, which is worth waiting for, the single sun-shaft through the bull's-eye that fumbles round the empty dome and withdraws.

Once at Chartres, when the big organ was being repaired, we got leave to go out on the roof and look at the reverse of the windows. We found that every square millimetre of the glass had been microscopically etched by the years: inlaid here with fine lines of dirt blown up from the street; roughened in places to a tooth-like rough drawing-paper or rubbed down to the silky softness of uncut diamond; studded with minute iridescent efflorescences and conchoidal pittings, and everywhere worked into a thousand varying planes to sift and glorify the light. So we saw that it is not Man that makes perfections but the weather which his works must endure. Those were good journeys.

Years later, I came across another side of inexhaustible France. It was after the return of Alsace, when the Head Quarters of the Administration (what in English we should call "Government House") had been purged of Boche memories and refurnished in detail with tapestries, mirrors, carpets, porcelain, and the rest. It was of the best; of one period; superbly and officially French, and impressing itself on humanity as though it had been in place since Attila. (*Emprise morale* again!)

I asked a friend, an Alsatian General, whence the flood of material had come. "From Marianne," was the reply. "She has all sorts of things like these in her stocking – when she needs them. You have seen the Élysée?" "One sees nothing at the Élysée," I retorted, "except the backs of large Generals. Where has all this been stored? Who issues it? Above all, who has arranged it here?" "Not my business," said the General. "Ask Marianne."

My relations with that lady had been strained because I had "doubled" on some temporary bridge in the devastated area, and she, through her agents, had talked to me as though I would overthrow the Republic. But she is an unequalled housekeeper. Think what it must have been in the old days when Rome lavished the best she had on her first external possession – her beloved Provincia!

* * *

En ce coing sont les Saxons, Estrelins, Ostrogotz et Alemans, peuples jadis invincibles maintenant aber keist et subjuguez par ung petit homme estropie. Ils nous demandent vengeance, secours, restitution de leur premier bon sens et liberté anticque.
RABELAIS, Lv. IV.

Since the first need of the unrepentant sinner is to make "a face for himself," the first German manoeuvre for position in the real war was to uproot the idea of Boche responsibility for the not-wholly-successful preliminary campaign. This they achieved in their own country by furious outcries and legislative enactments. It is, I believe, now a criminal offence for a Boche to breathe a doubt of his country's innocence. (Read "La Guerre" for "L'Amour m'a refit use virginité", and it is Frau Marion Delorme who declaims now.) But their technique with the foreigner filled me with professional jealousy as a purveyor of fiction vastly inferior. Many of our people conformed to this pressure, for England alone had lost more than eight hundred thousand dead of physique and conviction, and a large number of living who had been crippled or laid aside. Their places were taken in the public eye and ear by defaitists, intellectualists, Socialists, Communists, women enfranchised, and those whom four years of repressed and contagious fear had tried too severely. To these the thesis of the relativity of war-guilt offered a door for escape from themselves. If the war had been a cosmic dog-fight into which the nations had been drawn by cosmic hysteria, then all who had assisted to weaken, distract, delay, and confuse their own country and to encourage the enemy were, indeed, the martyr-souls and prophets they had believed themselves to be. They could sleep at last with approving consciences, and wake to demand for what the war had been fought. (It was, of course, that their species might survive to achieve office, honour, and influence.)

A certain amount of the same gas was liberated on the French front, but the national response was more feeble. The French were occupied with reconstruction, the gyrations of the franc, and, as in England, with strikes. Also they knew more than we did of the measures the Boche was taking to rehabilitate himself materially. He borrowed on all sides to recondition his untouched factories and his quite adequate railways. This interested the United States enormously. They are even more interested to-day, but not so polite. I am no financial expert, but a gentleman with a camion in charge of four enormous white sows with golden hair whom I overtook on the Digne-Grenoble road was good enough to explain the system. "Yes. He will borrow from all who will lend, and they will *all* go the same way. There is a fellow in our village doing the same thing. This is how he pays his debts. It is high finance. What you and I call civil banditry." That perspicacious pig-breeder spoke sitting between his four ladies, who looked like fat goddesses in *Orphée au Enfers*. He was more accurate than any expert.

There is a belief that the French are narrow and vindictive. It may be true, but the same man who would consider a wireless cabinet a wicked waste, tunes in to all European wavelengths. England is like a ship moored off a mainland which we visit occasionally. We do not feel at Calais that the earth under foot vibrates sustainedly as far as Vladivostock, Dantzig, and the far South. It is, I think, his continentality of experience and intuition that gives the Frenchman his unshaken poise irrespective of the circumstances or office at the moment; his power of useful words, his cynicism, and, above all, the quality of his humour.

After the stabilisation of the franc[4] and the general reduction of personnel and salaries organised by Monsieur Poincaré, I wished to hear from him the human effect of the measure. "It has been as one would expect," said he. "All the Préfets of all the Departments are running about telling their subordinates that, if the affair had rested with them, they would have increased all

---

[4] Though I lost some money by it, and had been severely reprehended during the war for hinting that it was inevitable, I could not but admire the pudicity of France's four-fifths repudiation. Do you remember the line in *Monsieur, Madame, et Bébé*, "Protect me, O Lord, but do not protect me too much"?

salaries. Then they say, 'But it is that Poincaré! Do you know the old brute? No? Well, I *do*. He is impossible – him and his idea!' And after all that is what I have been put here for."

And, apropos to our English system of business by cheque which makes our taxation so disgustingly effective, he furnished an illustration. "Do you know what a litre jar is? Yes, it holds a litre; but it can also hold ten thousand francs in small paper. You fill one with your economies. Then you bury it. Then you begin to fill another. That is all. In the villages now, men say of their richer neighbours, 'He must be at least a two- or three-jar man.' No! It is not so easy to collect taxes when the money is *there*!" And the square thumb was turned towards the carpet.

I love that imperturbable Lorrainer.

Towards the end of his life, Clemenceau, who had honoured me with his friendship, permitted me to report myself to him when I came through Paris. On the last occasion he was completing, I believe, some personal records, and the twilight into which he retired was alive and populous. He talked to himself as much as to me, ranging from Theirs and Gambetta and a picturesque duel of Rochefort's, to the statesmen of the present. He had caught malaria in Calcutta, and the doctors there administered medicines "out of bottles of the same pattern as my great-great-grandmother used. They said if I went North by train, I should die. I said, 'Then I will go North, and if necessary I will die in your accursed trains'. But, you see, I lived."

"That was because of the medicine in the bottles," I ventured.

"It was not. It was because I was so angry with the bottles!" He threw himself back and laughed. (I should not have dared to dose The Tiger when he was enjoying a temperature.)

That made me bold to ask, "And, now, Master, how do you

think of men as you have dealt with them and they with you in all these years?"

The answer came slowly. "Yes. I have known men? ... Yes. I have known them. ... They are not so bad. ... After all these years? ... They are not so bad after all."

There was the English handshake and then the accolade, as it had been in the office of *L'Homme Enchaîné* a thousand years ago.

And these are some of the reasons why I love France.

MY BOY JACK

"Have you news of my boy Jack?"
 Not this tide.
"When d'you think that he'll come back?"
Not with this wind blowing, and this tide.
"Has any one else had word of him?"
Not this tide.
For what is sunk will hardly swim,
Not with this wind blowing, and this tide.
"Oh, dear, what comfort can I find?"
None this tide,
Nor any tide,
Except he did not shame his kind—-
Not even with that wind blowing, and that tide.
Then hold your head up all the more,
This tide,
And every tide;
Because he was the son you bore,
And gave to that wind blowing and that tide.

ABOUT THE AUTHOR

Rudyard Kipling was born in Bombay, India, in 1865. He was sent to boarding school in England but returned to India as a young man, working as a journalist and writing poetry in fiction in his spare time. His first novel, *Plain Tales from the Hills*, was published to some acclaim in 1888.

After marrying the American, Caroline Baluster, in 1892, Kipling moved to Vermont and he and his wife had two daughters. It was here that he wrote *The Jungle Book*. However, following arguments with his wife's family, the Kiplings left America and settled in Sussex where a third child, a son, John, was born in 1897.

In 1902, the family moved into Bateman's, a 17th century house in East Sussex, where Kipling was to live for the rest of his life. His career as a writer went from strength to strength during this period and he became one of the most popular authors in the English language. He generally shunned honours, though, turning down both a knighthood and the position of Poet Laureate. He did, however, accept the Nobel Prize for Literature in 1907, becoming the first English author to receive the award.

Kipling's life was not without its hardship and tragedy. His daughter, for whom he had written the *Just So Stories*, died of pneumonia aged six, and his son, John, was killed in active service at the Battle of Loos during World War One.

Rudyard Kipling died in 1936 at the age of 70. He is buried in Poet's Corner in Westminster Abbey.

VERY SHORT CLASSICS

This book is part of the 'Very Short Classics' series, a collection of short books from around the world and across the centuries, many of which are being made available as ebooks, and paperbacks, for the very first time.

Also available in the Very Short Classics series…

THE FOUR DEVILS by Herman Bang

A classic of Danish literature.

When their mother drowns, young brothers Fritz and Adolf are sold into the circus by their grandmother, for a mere twenty marks. There they suffer under the cruel hand of Father Cecchi but are befriended by sisters Aimée and Louise and together they create an acrobatic act.

When Cecchi dies and the circus disbands, the quartet find there is little demand for acrobats and they refine their skills, re-emerging at The Four Devils, death-defying trapeze artists. Soon they are the talk of Europe, flying high from one city to another.

But one of the Four Devils, Aimée, finds that her feelings for Fritz have outgrown that of a sibling love and become a passion that pervades her every waking moment. So when Fritz begins an affair with an aristocratic heiress, Aimée's heart is broken and tensions threaten to also break the Four Devils apart, forever.

The Four Devils is a short novella from one of Denmark's most acclaimed writers.

CHILDLESS by Ignát Herrmann

A classic Czech novella.

When Ivan Hron is expelled from university because of his political beliefs he is kicked out of the family home and disinherited by his father. He finds a job in Prague as a bank clerk, works hard and impresses his employers. Some years later, he is appointed manager.

Now a man of considerable means he is keen to get married and start a family. One summer holiday he meets Magdalena, a young woman from the country who is at the resort with her parents, and falls in love. But his proposal of marriage is refused.

Six months pass and Ivan hears that Magda's father has fallen upon hard times. He gets back in touch, repeats his proposal and this time is accepted. And although their union is seemingly a happy one, it remains childless, much to Ivan's distress.

One day, Ivan discovers a letter his wife has hidden from him. The contents shatter his illusions of their happy marriage and reveal secrets that challenge everything he has hoped for in life.

But his reaction will surprise those around him and, quite possibly, the reader too.

Childless is a short novella by a revered Czech writer whose work is little-known in English. Its forward-thinking philosophy, way ahead of its time, makes it a story that deserves a modern readership.

This edition first published by Very Short Classics 2018

Copyright © Very Short Classics 2018

All rights reserved. No part of this publication may be reproduced, stored or transmitted in any form or by any means, electronic, mechanical, photocopying, recording, scanning, or otherwise without written permission from the publisher. It is illegal to copy this book, post it to a website, or distribute it by any other means without permission.

Originally published by Macmillan & Co. in 1933

ISBN: 979-8655345805

This book was professionally typeset on Reedsy. Find out more at reedsy.com

Printed in Poland
by Amazon Fulfillment
Poland Sp. z o.o., Wrocław